Exploring British Values

Democracy

Catherine Chambers

raintree

a Capstone company — publishers for children

Raintree is an imprint of Capstone Global Library Limited, a company incorporated in England and Wales having its registered office at 264 Banbury Road, Oxford, OX2 7DY – Registered company number: 6695582

www.raintree.co.uk
myorders@raintree.co.uk

Edited by Linda Staniford
Designed by Terri Poburka
Picture research by Pam Mitsakos
Original illustrations © Capstone Global Library Limited 2018
Illustrated by Graham Ross
Production by Steve Walker
Originated by Capstone Global Library
Printed and bound in China

ISBN 978 1 474 74077 7
21 20 19 18 17
10 9 8 7 6 5 4 3 2 1

British Library Cataloguing in Publication Data
A full catalogue record for this book is available from the British Library.

Acknowledgements
We would like to thank the following for permission to reproduce photographs: Alamy: Dinendra Haria, 29, Everyday Images, 11, Michael Kemp, 20-21, PA Images, 17, 27, Simon Dack News, 18; Getty Images: Dan Kitwood-WPA Pool, 15; iStockphoto: asiseeit, cover bottom; Newscom: ANDY RAIN/EPA, 12; Shutterstock: Arsenie Krasnevsky, 24-25, Attitude, design element, Ermine, design element, Lenscap Photography, 23, Lifestyle_Studio, design element, Richie Chan, 4-5, Sarunyu_foto, design element, URRRA, design element; Thinkstock: Photos.com, 7; Wikimedia: Arpingstone, 8- 9 bottom middle

We would like to thank Marguerite Heath, Programmes Director at the Citizenship Foundation, for her invaluable help in the preparation of this book.

Contents

Some words are shown in bold, **like this**. You can find out what they mean by looking in the glossary.

What is democracy?

Democracy means that each person in a country has the right to help make decisions. Britain is a democratic country, which means that adults can choose the people who make its laws and policies. Policies are plans on issues that affect all our lives, such as education. Democracy also means that each of us has the right to discuss policies and issues freely.

Democracy is a British value

Democracy is one of four key British values. These values help people to understand how to behave.

Get INVOLVED!

Draw up a list of decisions that you think are important to your school or community. See if your ideas change as you read this book.

The Task Team investigates

Amina, Emily and Kwame are the Task Team. They report on school and community issues for their class. This time, the team investigates democracy through a local incident.

This piece of land was a great gift to the community.

WE WANT A PEACE GARDEN

WE NEED A PLAY GROUND

Yes. But who decides what to do with it?

Yes, it seems that older people want a garden.

And parents with kids want a playground!

RENFIELD CARE HOME for the ELDERLY

Parliament and the people

In Britain, we choose, or elect, people to make decisions about our local communities. These people are local **councillors** and they make decisions at local council meetings. We elect other people to make decisions about our country. They are called **Members of Parliament** (MPs). MPs attend our House of Commons, in Parliament.

Most adults in Britain can vote at local and national elections. They vote for the person they believe has the best policies and will do the best job.

Around the world

About 60 per cent of countries in the world are democracies. Each of these countries has its own form of government and democratic system for choosing its representatives.

The enormous buildings of the Houses of Parliament are in a part of London called Westminster.

It's not just about us kids. And the land's not big enough for both.

PLAYGROUND!

PLAYGROUND!

PLAYGROUND!

The journey to democracy

A thousand years ago, Britain was divided into smaller kingdoms. The rulers of these kingdoms had total power over their people. Then, over 800 years ago in England, wealthy barons became angry at the king's powers. They forced King John I to sign a charter, or list, of people's rights. This was called Magna Carta. The journey to democracy had begun.

Different points of view

From 1327, Parliament included knights, who represented each town or county. But the idea of letting every adult have their say was not considered until 1647. Then, a group called the Levellers published "The Agreement of the People". In it, they proposed that every adult man should have a vote. Parliament rejected the Levellers' ideas at this time.

Power to all people

In 1707, Scotland joined England and Wales to form the United Kingdom of Great Britain. Yet only rich men were allowed to represent all these nations in Parliament. By the end of the 1800s, less-wealthy working men could also vote, if they rented property of a set value. There was no mention of women.

In the early 1900s a group of women called the suffragettes began to fight for women's equality. They wanted the same rights for men and women, especially the right to vote.

Finally, in 1918, all men over 21 years of age and women over 30 were allowed to vote. Women over 21 could vote only in 1928. Then in 1969 the Representation of the People Act reduced the voting age to 18.

Over 100 years ago, women called suffragettes marched and fought for the right to vote.

Democracy and us

In Britain, we choose representatives who make plans and laws that affect us all. So it is important to understand what they do. This knowledge helps us decide whom to vote for in elections. It helps us to think through the decisions we have to make in our own lives. We learn how they affect people around us.

Decisions for the country

The British government makes decisions and passes laws that matter to the whole country. It decides on issues concerning the environment, agriculture, transport, health, education and housing. It also decides on foreign **policy**, which is how we deal with other countries.

Policies, or aims, for each issue are drawn up in a department, with a Minister at its head. Examples are the Department for Education and the Department for Culture, **Media** and Sport.

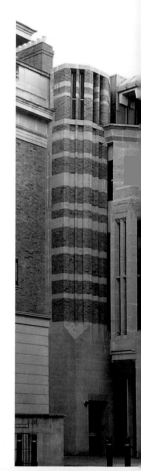

Decisions in our community

Local **politicians** are chosen to meet together on their town, district or city council. Here, they make decisions about their local area. Their plans affect our streets, schools, housing, hospitals, parks, libraries, local transport and sports facilities.

Fact FILE

Britain's government has 25 departments, each with its own Minister. Find out what they are. Do you think that some are more important than others? If so, why?

Richmond House is where Ministers and civil servants run the Department of Health.

RICHMOND HOUSE 79 WHITEHALL

YOU Decide!

What issues are important to you? If you had to create a new department, what would it be and why? You could discuss this with others, or conduct a survey.

YEAH! WE WANT A PLAYGROUND!

But it's a LOCAL piece of land, for EVERYONE.

We don't even know how much it will cost to clear the land.

True. Task Team! I think you should FIND OUT!

Deciding how money is spent

When we vote, we have to make a lot of choices. One of them is how we want our government or local council to spend the nation's money. An important part of **democracy** is choosing politicians who we think will spend wisely. Politicians often do not agree on how money should be spent.

Where does the money come from?

We all have to pay for the things we have or do. Each government department also has to pay for what it does, and each receives money from central government. The government gets this money through **taxation**. The government takes tax from working people's wages and from businesses, such as factories and shops.

Managing our money

The amount of money the government has to spend is called the Total Managed Expenditure (TME). It is also called the **budget**. If you receive pocket money, the amount you have to spend is your budget. Your school has a budget, too.

On our doorstep

Local councils spend money on the things we see all around us, such as schools and hospitals. They receive some money from the government. They receive the rest through taxation from local residents and businesses.

Local councils spend money making our parks and gardens enjoyable spaces.

Get INVOLVED!

How is money spent in your school? Are there different budgets such as Heating and Lighting, Reading Books or Sports Equipment? If you receive pocket money, you could divide your spending into budgets, too.

Making plans

We all make plans and take decisions. Most of us want our plans and decisions to be good for us, and fair to the people around us. In a **democracy**, the government tries to do this too.

People are protesting outside the Houses of Parliament about new railway plans called High Speed 2 (HS2).

Not so fast! The whole community must help decide what to do with the land.

Or we won't get the money?

EXACTLY!

Who should benefit from plans?

In a democracy, we should all benefit from our government's plans. However, each government department has a **budget**. The plans for each department should not cost more than the budget. Some departments have good ideas but they may cost too much and cannot be achieved. Not all departments will be pleased with the amount they receive.

Different issues

For example, a new railway planned to run through five towns might be too expensive. Instead, the Department of Transport could decide that the railway should only run through three towns. This means that two towns would lose out. At the same time, some people might think that the railway will spoil the environment and will not want it at all. Each plan has many issues.

Get INVOLVED!

Research and discuss the issues around the following plans for Britain:

1. The plan to expand Heathrow Airport by building a third runway.
2. The plan to build High Speed 2, which would be the UK's second high-speed railway line.

Freedom to challenge

In a democracy, it is our right to give our point of view. In the case above, we might sign an online petition to the government about the plans. Or we might write an email or letter to the Minister for Transport, who is in charge of the department. We can also write to our local **Member of Parliament**.

Discussion is a part of democracy

Most plans we make are easy, such as going to work or school every day. Some are much more difficult, and we need to discuss these with other people. Our government also takes part in discussions when it makes new plans or takes important decisions.

Sitting together

Many of us discuss our work, plans and challenges together around a table. It gives other people a chance to join in and give their opinion. Our government does this too.

The **Prime Minister**, who leads the government, sits at a table with ministers from each government department. This is known as the **Cabinet**. The Cabinet meets at No. 10 Downing Street in London, the home of the Prime Minister. Here, the Prime Minister and his or her ministers make plans but the final decisions are made by the people chosen to represent the whole of Britain in Parliament.

YOU Decide!

How easy is it to give someone good advice? Can you just use facts to help find what is best for them? Or do you let your personal opinion creep into the argument? It isn't easy!

There's a lot to find out before the meeting.

Yes, the land's so overgrown we can't even measure it!

Ah! We can now! The council's Planning Department has sent us diagrams.

Getting advice

You might ask a responsible adult or trusted friends to give you good advice. Ministers ask experts from a large body of advisors called the **Civil Service**. We cannot vote for these advisors. So it is important that their opinions are based on facts, not personal opinion.

Prime Minister Theresa May (centre) is holding a Cabinet meeting with her most important ministers near her.

I'm really excited! Our project involves the whole community.

Yes, everyone can give their ideas. Everyone has a vote.

Archie! We need your art skills to make a massive model of the land.

WHY?!

You'll see!

15

Debating and deciding

We often need to share our plans, especially when they affect other people. In our **democracy**, the government shares its plans, too. The **Prime Minister** and Ministers present their plans, called **Bills**, to Parliament. It is here that our chosen **Members of Parliament** (MPs) decide which Bills become law.

Democracy means getting opinions

Each government plan is written as a Draft Bill. Draft means that it is still only an idea. It needs further discussion, usually by a special committee.

Sometimes a Draft Bill needs a wider view. So it is published in a **Green Paper**. This means that our MPs and the public can offer advice. The government then publishes a firmer, clearer plan, called a **White Paper**. Experts can offer their opinions on a White Paper.

All the ideas in the Draft Bill and Papers are then taken to Parliament for full debate. Afterwards, the Bill is revised and taken again to Parliament. Here, the government hopes it will be passed.

What is Parliament?

Britain's Parliament consists of the Crown, which is our king or queen, the House of Commons and the House of Lords. Each Bill is debated first in the House of Commons, where our elected MPs sit. Most Bills are then discussed in the House of Lords, where members are not elected. The final vote goes to our MPs in the House of Commons. The king or queen signs the Bill so that it becomes an **Act of Parliament**. This means that it is now a law.

MPs are listening quietly in the House of Commons. Sometimes they shout and heckle!

Fact FILE

Debate in Parliament can get very noisy! Democracy means we should listen, too. The debates are controlled by the **Speaker** of the House. He or she is an MP, who is selected by all the other MPs.

Land Meeting

There! I think flowers will look just right...here.

Yes. A great idea!

I thought you wanted a park!

It isn't about what I want. It's what MOST people want.

Choosing our representatives

In a democracy, we can change our ideas sometimes. About every four years, we get the chance to change our **politicians** in a General Election, or **ballot**. Having the opportunity to vote for change is important in our democracy.

Our chosen MPs usually belong to political parties, whose members agree on most issues. The two largest parties in Britain are the Conservative Party and the Labour Party. In a General Election, the party that receives the most votes governs the country and makes new plans.

During an election, ballot boxes are emptied and votes are counted.

A wider democracy

Scotland, Wales and Northern Ireland have their own parliaments, but MPs from those countries also have to attend and vote in the House of Commons. This gives them more power over their issues.

At a local level, we vote for local politicians who sit on our local council. Most local **councillors** belong to the same political parties as MPs.

Democractic voting also works on a local level through the elections of important community figures. These include school governors, club leaders and presidents of local associations.

Election day!

Elections for MPs and councillors are held on a single day, from 7 a.m. to 10 p.m. They take place at local **polling stations**. Here, people poll, or vote, for their chosen person, or candidate.

At polling stations, people pick up a ballot paper and mark a cross against the name of their candidate. They do this in secret, so that no one can check who they have voted for. Then they post the paper in a locked ballot box.

All ballot boxes are taken to large halls across the country. Here, they are unlocked and the votes counted. Election night can be very exciting!

Get INVOLVED!

Do you have a school council? If not, you might want to make a plan to set one up and present it to your head teacher.

Actually, they're watching the whole thing on video.

And they've got their own ballot box.

We're counting email votes, too.

And some people are posting their vote.

PEACE   CHILDREN'S

Is Parliament perfect democracy?

We rely on politicians to help sort out problems where we live, but they also have to sort out problems that concern the whole of the UK. However, people who we do not vote for also make decisions. Is this **democracy**?

These decision makers are not elected

As we have seen, Parliament is also made up of members of the House of Lords, who are not elected. The **Prime Minister** who leads our government is chosen by his or her political party. Some people think that this does not matter. Others say it is not democratic.

It is our right to think about and discuss our democracy. Does it work for most people? Does it need to change?

Yes or No?

Sometimes there is a very important question that people want to decide for themselves. If Parliament agrees, an election is held just for that one issue. This is called a **referendum**. A secret ballot is held and each voter puts a cross against a "Yes" or a "No" answer to the issue.

The question asked in a referendum is usually very simple but the issue might be very complicated. Is a referendum the right way of deciding an answer to a complicated problem?

People who wanted Britain to remain in the EU lost the vote in a **referendum**. But they can still make their point.

I WANT TO BE IN EU

YOU *Decide!*

Do we behave in a democratic way in our community or at school? Is there an important issue in your community or school that you think could be decided by a referendum?

It's certainly democratic. But choosing between two different plans divided our community.

Well. I've been talking to a lot of Peace Garden voters. We'd actually thought of having a Community Garden for EVERYONE!

Freedom of expression

We learn about local and national issues through the **media**. We rely on the media to give us the facts. This can be difficult because information is researched and gathered in different ways. It is used for different purposes. Opinions are often presented as facts, and are later proved to be wrong. This can lead to "fake news".

Fair information

Under our **democracy** we enjoy **freedom of expression**, which means the freedom to speak and write our opinions. This includes our opinions about our government, whether good or bad. We can speak freely in public on the radio, television or internet. We can write freely in the press, which means books, newspapers and digital media.

Our media sometimes uses opinions to present both sides of an argument. Media headlines can use emotional language rather than facts to grab our attention. This is confusing and makes it difficult to decide which side we agree with.

Headlines grab a reader's attention but do not necessarily tell the whole truth.

Get INVOLVED!

Find the facts about an important issue that you and others feel strongly about. Get together and write some newspaper articles giving different points of view, with persuasive but factual headlines.

Let's keep calm and use our networks.

Yes. Let's get the TRUE story out through OUR blog and 'Classroom Gazette'

CLASSROOM GAZETTE

HEY!' This email says the council's seen the report. And WE'VE GOT THE FUNDING!

Our democratic values and the world

There are many different ideas about **democracy** around the world. Some come from other countries. Others come from international organisations such as the **United Nations (UN)**.

Learning from others

We can learn from other ideas on democracy. We might not agree with all of them. But studying them helps us to keep thinking about British democracy. We can see if our democracy works well in a modern world. We can understand that no democracy is perfect, not even our own.

We can look at the UN's guidelines on democracy to check that our own is working. Democracy is a key value of the UN, just as it is in Britain.

Democracy is one of the values laid down in the United Nations Declaration of Human Rights. This declaration asks countries to treat their citizens equally and with **respect**. It asks them to allow their citizens to enjoy freedom and choice, which includes taking part in elections.

This UN building is in Geneva, Switzerland. The largest UN building is in New York, USA.

The United Nations was set up in 1945. It was created to repair the damage after World War II (1939–1945) and set up a system of values. It now has 193 member states. Not all have democracies like ours.

Countries without a democracy

People in some countries do not have free and fair elections. They do not have **freedom of expression**. Sometimes, a government holds elections but ignores the results if it does not win.

Do our democratic values work?

British democracy lets everyone have a voice. Yet it is not always fair to all of us. There are winners and losers.

Is our democracy fair?

Many of us want all British people to have equal chances and choices. This is hard to achieve because Britain's wealth is not spread out equally. There are some people who do not think equality is important at all. These people can choose politicians who represent their beliefs. So democracy means choice but at the moment does not necessarily mean fairness to all.

Do our elections represent our whole population?

Women make up just over half of Britain's population. Yet in the 2015 General Election, only 191 women were chosen as MPs in the House of Commons. This is 29 per cent of all Britain's 650 MPs. The **United Nations** urges governments across the world to give women equal opportunities in all areas of life, including politics.

About 13 per cent of British people come from ethnic minority communities. Yet only 6 per cent are MPs. This means that we do not get a full range of views in government. We do not get a complete picture of life in Britain.

Democracy is not just for government. You might like to set up or join a debating society. This gives confidence in expressing ideas and opinions. You can discuss issues that are fun as well as serious!

Britain's Youth Parliament of children aged 11 to 18 gets the chance to debate issues in the House of Commons.

The future for British democracy

British **democracy** is not perfect but it is a value that we can all help to improve. We can use democratic values in our daily lives. We can listen, and speak freely but fairly. We can take part in debate on important issues and stand up for the rights of others.

Democracy and British identity

Our democratic system has developed over 800 years and has faced a lot of challenges along the way. Some of our kings and queens ignored it while others tried to stop some of their citizens from taking part. Today, most of us take pride in our democratic values and systems, which have become a part of who we are.

Forcing us to vote – is this democracy?

Forcing people to vote is just one of many future concerns. Should we force people to take part in elections or is this against our democratic right to choose? In some countries, such as Australia, voting is compulsory.

YOU Decide!

Should 16-year-olds be given the chance to vote? This is a hot topic. You debate and you decide!

I've got lots of feedback for you on the Community Garden.

Well, we're here to learn and improve!

Thank you for coming. D'you think the Community Garden's a success?

YES!. And that's what happens when everybody LISTENS!

The 2016 referendum

In the **referendum**, voters could vote "Yes" or "No" to leaving the European Union, a European economic organization. Almost 46.5 million voters could have voted. Just over 33.5 million actually did. In the end, about 17.5 million decided that Britain should leave the EU. This is less than one third of those who could have voted. The referendum has raised questions about our democracy that will continue for a long time.

Teenagers under 18 show how much they want the right to vote. In a democracy, they can protest in this way.

OUR FUTURE OUR VOTE

OUR FUTURE OUR CHOICE

WE HAD NO CHOICE GIVE US A VOICE

COMMUNITY GARDEN

FEEDBACK

It's Mrs Carey – the COUNCIL OFFICER!

Oh NO! Maybe they're going to take away the funding!

Don't look so worried! The council wants to know what's NEXT for the Community Garden!

Come inside and see!

Glossary

Act of Parliament Bill that has been approved by both Houses of Parliament and by the reigning monarch (Royal Assent) so that it becomes law

ballot secret voting

Bill proposal for a new law, to be debated in Parliament

budget estimate of expected income and expenditure over the coming year

Cabinet group of senior ministers chosen by the Prime Minister to discuss important topics

Civil Service people who work for the administrative sections of the government of a country

councillor member of a local council, who makes decisions at a local level

democracy type of government in which the people elect their leaders

freedom of expression the right to express opinions freely through speech, writing and other methods

Green Paper first draft of a report on a particular topic, for discussion by MPs and the public. If it is accepted it is made into a more final document called a White Paper.

media means of mass communication, such as newspapers, radio, TV and the Internet

Member of Parliament (MP) person elected by people living in a particular area to represent them in the House of Commons

policy course of action followed by a government

politician person who holds a political office

polling station place where people go to vote during an election

Prime Minister (PM) leader of the Government; the leader of the party that wins a general election. The Prime Minister lives at 10, Downing Street in London.

referendum public vote to decide a question

respect accept that someone has certain rights

Speaker MP who has been chosen by other MPs to control debates in the House of Commons

taxation collecting money from people and businesses to support government policies

United Nations (UN) international organization formed to keep peace in the world and to defend human rights

White Paper Government proposal for a new law, for discussion. If a White Paper is accepted it is made into a Bill and discussed in Parliament.

Find out more

Books

You might like to look at these other books on British Values:

BREXIT: Britain's Decision to Leave the European Union, Dan Nunn (Raintree, 2017)

Democracy (Systems of Government), Sean Connolly (Franklin Watts, 2017)

Let's Vote on it! (British Values), Christopher Yeates (Gresham Books, 2016)

What Does It Mean to be British?, Nick Hunter (Raintree, 2017)

Websites

www.bbc.co.uk/newsround
The CBBC Newsround website gives lots of interesting features on rights and values around the world.

www.bbc.co.uk/newsround/30880972
You can watch a video about Parliament on this site.

www.un.org/en/universal-declaration-human-rights/
On this site you can read the United Nations Declaration of Human Rights.

Index